WE

(THE PEOPLE OF THE UNITED STATES)

Also by Joshua Bennett

POETRY

The Study of Human Life

Owed

The Sobbing School

NONFICTION

Spoken Word: A Cultural History

Being Property Once Myself: Blackness and the End of Man

The People Can Fly: American Promise, Black Prodigies, and the Greatest Miracle of All Time

WE

(THE PEOPLE OF THE UNITED STATES)

Joshua Bennett

PENGUIN POETS

PENGUIN BOOKS
An imprint of Penguin Random House LLC
1745 Broadway, New York, NY 10019
penguinrandomhouse.com

Set in Adobe Caslon Pro
Designed by Sabrina Bowers

LIBRARY OF CONGRESS CATALOGING-IN-PUBLICATION DATA
Names: Bennett, Joshua (Poet) author
Title: We (the people of the United States) / Joshua Bennett.
Description: New York : Penguin Poets, 2026. | Series: Penguin poets
Identifiers: LCCN 2025043952 (print) | LCCN 2025043953 (ebook) |
ISBN 9780143138648 paperback | ISBN 9780593512753 ebook
Subjects: LCGFT: Poetry
Classification: LCC PS3602.E664483 W48 2026 (print) | LCC PS3602.E664483 (ebook)
LC record available at https://lccn.loc.gov/2025043952
LC ebook record available at https://lccn.loc.gov/2025043953

Printed in the United States of America

The authorized representative in the EU for product safety and compliance is Penguin Random House Ireland, Morrison Chambers, 32 Nassau Street, Dublin D02 YH68, Ireland, https://eu-contact.penguin.ie.

for all my people

Acknowledgments

Sincerest thanks to the following journals for publishing earlier versions of the poems featured in this book:

AGNI: "First Philosophy" and "It Runs in the Family"

American Poetry Review: "Anchorage, Alaska," "Hanover, New Hampshire," "Hawthorne, California," "Lynchburg, Virginia," and "Yonkers, New York"

Best American Poetry: "First Philosophy"

Harvard Review: "We"

Places Journal: "Essay on Trees"

Poetry: "Physical Education" and "We"

The Southern Review: "Chapel Hill, North Carolina" and "Decatur, Alabama"

Yale Review: "Eatonville, Florida"

Thank you, always, to the ancestors and elders who have left this mortal plane, and will never be forgotten: Grandma, Uncle Gene, Uncle Stanley, Auntie, and Cousin Tanya. Thank you to the family who raised me up, and appear more than once in these pages: Toya, Mom, Dad, Levi. Our story is yet unfolding.

To my friends, thank you for standing with me in times of both celebration and mourning, and helping me get this book out into the world: Thomas Alston, Jamil Baldwin, Andrea Bossi, Jamall Calloway, Devin Chamberlain, Mary Fuller, Danielle Georges, Carlos Andrés Gomez, Wilfredo Gomez, Florence Ladd, Susan Lambe Sariñana, Wesley J. Morris, Gavin Moses, Imani Perry, Therí Pickens, Ronald Johnson, Rodney Reynolds, Patrick Sylvain, and Daniella Toosie-Watson.

Sincerest thanks to A. S. Kline for his translation of Virgil's *Georgics*, and to Susan Stewart for sharing these poems with me many years ago.

Thank you, most of all, to my wife and children: Pam, August, and June. Your love is my life's greatest joy and reward.

Contents

not so much looking for the shape
as being available
to any shape that may be
summoning itself
through me
from the self not mine but ours.

—A. R. AMMONS

An old man said this thing to me:
"The loveliest word of all is 'we.'"

—GWENDOLYN BROOKS, AGE 17

I.

WE

FIRST PHILOSOPHY

What is your all-time favorite
phenomenon? Mine is when
the error is as lovely as the aim.

The other day, my wife texts me, *Love*
thy baby, like a contemporary
commandment. Later, she explains

that she meant to write *Love that baby*,
in response to a Mint Condition song
I sent that morning, but I can't let

the first phrase go. It reminds me of those
older saints on Sunday saying *Look at God*
whenever they were interrupted

by transcendent beauty. I tried & did not
see Him, nor dare to ask where I might
search. But I cherished the lesson; took

personally that charge to study the invisible,
call forward its power through chant or speech,
a distinct vocal pattern or arrangement of keys,

& the spirit would cast its fathomless cloak
over us. Make us glow. At home, we worshipped
precision: children honed by hot combs & ironing

boards, perfect grades, our family name
a banner we carried in our war against
the outside world. How did I get here?

This soft blue house in Massachusetts,
my hand against the Japanese maple
outside to better hear its wisdom,

son singing ballads in his toddler Esperanto
downstairs, as I try to compose the story
of our arrival—getting the details wrong,

no doubt, though that melody
is unmistakable, clear—from all those
dreams, dueling, in the air.

WE

We grew up listening to the gossip
of elders in crowded salons, the Holy

Spirit, Hot 97, our gut's drum
major signaling whether to run

left or right when a bullet's ricochet
cracked the nighttime air. Jokes

about our hair; Mama's weight;
our place in the great graph

of human potential. We slap-
boxed until it turned to scrap

-ping unexpectedly, scuffles
blossoming from schoolyard

play we claimed was meant to
enhance precision, little else.

We had no good words for wealth; no
trust in arbitrary rules, or sense of power

beyond the kinds that shaped our lives
inside discernible bounds: the belt,

the badge, shoeboxes underneath
the bed which held abuela's savings,

first poems, the heels our mothers
once wore to shuffle the shine off the floors

of a disco spot downtown, where working
people went to let the stress of day,

last shift's weight, evaporate. We
knew the cool ambrosia of hydrant

water; how, without it, we might not have
survived the height of July's brutality. We learned

Spanish to talk to girlfriends' mothers
via landline, ask permission to speak

for a half hour after school, *para discutir*
la tarea, or some other benevolent, though

transparently false, claim. We dreamt
of flight, and heavyweight fights, and playing

our latest hits on late night TV, crossing
up small forwards on the *NBA on NBC*

with our uncles watching, their
voices so loud the neighbors

assumed someone must have lost
a bet. We imagined a world without

debt, or early death, or stress so heavy
the mind must be lifted elsewhere

to bear it and yet persist. We
were latchkey kids, troubadours,

substitute parents at fourteen,
teaching little brothers to read

and long divide, and ride
the bus home alone in time to reach

the front door just before dark,
when the world put on another face

so we did too, and with masks
and wigs we got from Grandma

devised productions to fill the day's
remainder, command the language

we inherited to live anew, or else
fail magnificently at trying to say

what we held most dear, but could not
yet sketch onto the palimpsest

of the world
as we knew it.

IT RUNS IN THE FAMILY

like horses through the smoke
of a field on fire. We dance
in its light, which has surrounded

us since we were born & grown
in intensity ever since. My brothers
& I occupy separate bricks

of the same bridge: outside
the scripts we learned in school
for ways that human thinking

blooms. Or should. Our neighbor
-hoods were laboratories,
their explosive effects embedded

in us, one might say, the way color
holds feeling. The basics of popular
Lockean dicta offer little to clarify

how I came to be here like this,
in this mind, upside
down. The doctor says

it runs in the family and doesn't
explain. The war runs in
my father's blood like arrows

through elk. Is that how you
mean? The prison runs in my
brother's blood like language

through an era. There is a boy alone
in a room, at a desk, at the bottom
of a pile, and the words run through

his brain when he hears you speak,
like a mutiny unspooling. We arrive
in this life with so much already

inscribed. I sing to my son *careful*
when he attempts to achieve liftoff.
Morrison's children were shocked

to learn they couldn't fly. As was I.

PHYSICAL EDUCATION

For the sake of argument, let's say
the day my father outlawed all contact
between backhand and face, back
-side and belt, stiletto cast like a harpoon

across the living room's auburn length
and the protagonist running toward the opposite
door, was a Thursday. And let's say the logic
of his claim went that if he & everyone else

in the house could hit me then, while I was still small,
I would one day grow to be a bomb like so many
brothers he'd seen held up & buried for tempers
flaring in open air. A beating now would be a book

-mark in my memory's eye; a black mark on the calendar
I kept inside; a day he would be made to meet me
in the square. Every little boy's brain keeps score. And who
among us hasn't been held, helpless, before? At the feet

of mercy or underneath them. From that day forward,
I was counters to every command, a conflagration
of untamed language, now detached from a program
of corporal might. The lesson took. I was tall as a man

the next time my father and I shook the house with
our rage and shame. We breathed like dancers,
and allowed our hostility to take its form,
my teenage fists honed in the outside world

where no one loves you enough
to let the boy back up when he loses,
grant him a moment to shake the dust,
knuckle up, try his luck, again.

ESSAY ON TREES

Last night, the big chestnut across the street was split in half, either by light
-ning or wind, I can't tell which. I'm only mortal. I slept
as the elements took their toll, and awakened to a neighbor
-hood freighted by debris, branches and leaves, ochre and scarlet
and hunter green, like a bag of jewels dumped over the mountainside.
The tree was bisected almost perfectly, as if by blade. It refused
to fall. Seeing it, I did not think of my own impermanence, though I do
now, recalling its obliviated majesty.

One of my favorite bands on planet Earth is called the War
on Drugs, and they are playing live on my computer screen
for the nineteen minutes I give myself to jot down this sense
of things, in part so as not to lose it. I hold my son up with one arm.
Talk to him about tone, inheritance. I want to add a footnote about
how the guitar in Adam Granduciel's hands comes from an elaborate
forest somewhere remote, where it is so dark the deer sprint across
the understory without conflict, imperceptible as atoms.

The boy needs strawberries, so we are off to Trader Joe's to forage
through boxes of discounted fruit, some just coming into the glory
of their season. Quietly, I await the apricots' summer return. Across the parking
lot there is a sporting goods store. I have plans to buy a red rowing boat
built for two. The schematics of another are already sketched in my mind;
a bright orange copy of *Boatbuilding* tucked away in the bookcase to keep me
honest. There is a love I walk inside as old as the invisible generations of oaks
and evergreens keeping us alive. They are my witnesses and brothers.
In the cathedral of their shadows, my dreams grow tall.

WE

The money of the mind is attention, maybe.
Which is not, initially, where I thought I'd begin,
but we're already here now, using the language
of care and economy, though God-talk was truly
my first way in. *Sustained attention is how we approach*
a flesh and blood experience of the Divine I say to the
therapist nodding her head, only moments after
we disagree over whether her dress is coral or yellow
-based red, as opposed, of course, to a blue-based
red, like the square on her tartan scarf. My jacket
is the color of snow on television. My eyes
are as brown as my father's when he lifted a stranger
off the ground he saw through the driver's-side window
beating a woman on Broadway. I am almost the age now
he was then, and am still studying the difference between
what a man proclaims in speech and what he says with his
body. Tomorrow marks another year on Earth for his third
son, and he is a father now, with a boy he is trying to teach
the benefits of apprehension. Who instead prefers to walk
on his hands, leap from the playground slide, climb
on countertops to watch TV from another room entirely.
Where does my influence, my aspiration, end and the child
begin? Who refashions the cosmos with his laughter.

II.

THE PEOPLE OF THE UNITED STATES

We owe each other everything.

—FRED MOTEN AND STEFANO HARNEY

YONKERS, NEW YORK

The Invocation (1–42)

God of fauna, fences, horsemint flower shards
thickening the wind in spring; God of future
tenses, forget-me-nots, fourth birthday wishes,
French translations of canonically American dishes
—e.g., the *pommes purée* I had in a Philadelphia hotel
restaurant once, made of potatoes instead of apples,
as in the myth of the McDonald's apple pie, and thus in its description
omitting the Earth—God of Earth and Mars, mirth, feldspar,
Allan Rohan Crite's *Streetcar Madonna*, God of chameleons
& iguanas, Komodo dragons, hawks, harriers, all living
dinosaur descendants; God of the remnant, & the luminous
golden pendants bearing photographs of grandmothers
that black men in New Orleans sometimes wear;
God of autumnal air, crisp as an axe-head against ice,
God of satellites, and the eternal sequence of combusting
celestial lights surrounding them, to which we hitch
our ruminations, even still, even this one, a penitent's prayer
in print: hear us, O God of the glint in the dark which is not
a blade, but a lover's eye reworking the castaway
threads of our solitary moon. God of the boom-
bap emanating from your big sister's room
that carries you an ocean away, and back,
just in time to decompress from the tragicomic
epiphanies that followed you home from school,
the waking dream of that singular mortality,
childhood, where you are a witness to the world
without weapons. God of prescience, omnipresence,
Christmas presents from aunts & uncles of such
immediate, practical use, they seem to defy

the ritual: crayons & pencils, pick-up sticks you play
with alongside your cousins for one day only,
rubber erasers the same shade as the peonies
in Grandma's bedside window—bubblegum-pink's Platonic
form—to remind you of what you already know:
it all goes. God of primrose, princes, printing presses
skipping songs like stones over the surface of human
consciousness, collected as if clouds in the invisible
coliseums just above our heads. God of water
-beds, bedlam, the peculiar shade of red in a boy's eyes
when what he loves begins to crack in half. God of pure math,
the sea's unchecked wrath, this untamed love, this reaching
out into the warmth of all that blue, and gray, without shame.

DECATUR, ALABAMA

1\.
Naturally, we begin with Sun Ra's escape pod arcing
through seamless indigo. Fleeing Saturn for Earth,
a Birmingham crash landing in 1914, thirty-four years
before my father enters atmosphere. Five in advance
of the day Klansmen slash the tires of Pop's bright orange
Firebird, parked just off campus; forever marking senior year
with an air of utopian striving—the open road a metonym
for life's million hidden prizes—cut just short. Twenty siblings,
two sets of ten, packed into four cars for shopping trips.
A quarter of them with eyes as green as Grandpa's, or God's.
Alabama, the roll call of your children reads like the first
ballot of blackness's hall of fame: King, Sanchez, Paige,
Walker, Mays, Joe Louis & John Lewis, Jesse Owens racing
the twilight home, Zora Neale Hurston summoning songs
from the mouths of mules and saints to hold up the sky.

2\.
for Mae Jemison

It was, perhaps, our oldest ritual:
my father & I watching *Star Trek*
on the living room floor, quiet

as calculation, my small frame
beside his own, like an image
& its draft. We studied any & all

variations of the show we adored
like no other: *Voyager*, *Deep Space Nine*,
The Next Generation, comparing each

iteration to its ancestor only once
it had run its course. I saw myself
everywhere: Data, Worf, Geordi

La Forge, scientists & warriors,
interstellar adventurers in any form
you could imagine, all comportments

welcome, central, to the mission
of the *Starship Enterprise*, my boyhood
eyes aglow as I dreamt

of gliding through the incandescent
blackness of the great beyond,
smooth as a scimitar, even

in hyperdrive, me & my intrepid
crew, cruising at light speed
toward the promise of another life.

Pop never explained the tradition.
But the call to see that story
unfolding was its own

inheritance, a journey through
outer galaxies as it was
through his own mind,

the stillness in that room
no issue for me, who knew
even then that quiet

had its own texture & richness,
that my father had always been this way,
a man who spoke with deeds, a look

in his eyes that could level
a room, or else lift it into orbit.
Over the years, he would teach me

many names: Benjamin Banneker,
Lewis H. Latimer, Mary McLeod
Bethune: narrators

of our heroic human drama. George
Washington Carver; Arthur Schomburg;
Mae Jemison, who I would later learn

was born in Alabama, just like Pop,
& loved *Star Trek* too, & was the first
black woman to reach outer space,

& the first real astronaut to ever go
on the show—*The Next Generation*, to be
exact—at the invitation of LeVar Burton,

who was already a hero in our household,
based on the transcendent power of *Reading
Rainbow* alone, but this was another level,

this woman who had held an audience
with the moon, seen the other side
of the atmosphere that held us here,

this dreamer of a human civilization
on Mars, this teacher, this healer, this
author of children's books & once

-distant goals made material for generations
of us told we would inherit nothing, & learn
to love that absence; instead, Dr. Jemison said,

the very cosmos could belong to us, the darkness
of our skin, our hair, our eyes, was shared
with that shimmering infinitude, that endless

breadth, the possibility that we too might
one day take flight, achieve the weightlessness
we had only felt in dreams, or heard

when we heard Whitney Houston sing,
or saw on TV in briefest flashes of stars
millions of miles beyond our own,

but more palpable now, so close you
could almost grasp them, almost hold
them there, in your palm, like a promise.

LYNCHBURG, VIRGINIA

The Beginnings of Agriculture (118–159)

with a line from Wendy Walters

Before Jupiter's time no farmers worked the land:
Or so we are told, though we must
imagine scores of poets honing songs
in sugar fields, underground, held
within the belly of ships, prophets
of an age before our inner worlds might
manifest on paper, and the sacred
bard behind the words survive. Hence,
the standard becomes subterfuge,
concealment, a century and a half
passes between Hammon's first lines
in print and Anne Spencer's "Questing,"
her timeless directive: *Let me learn now*
where Beauty is. And preserve it by whatever
means available, inventing new ones, even,
if the methods at hand are insufficient,
or require we lose our sense of what it means
to *amplify the life*, to see the boy in chains
and know there is an endlessness in him
the present obscures. At their home in Lynchburg,
Edward Spencer builds for his beloved
an enclosed garden, half an acre, where the titans
of their day meet and map another vision
of this world within the Veil: James Weldon
Johnson, Paul Robeson, W. E. B. Du Bois all
drink and dance, conjuring the future phrase
by phrase. And Anne, the chambers of her mind

filled with flowers, nasturtium and hollyhock,
germander, bergamot, turtlehead, butterfly
weed, book after book bursting with petals
and stems she shares with the children levitating
through the library at Dunbar High School,
where she guards meticulously the rolling record
of our travails & overcoming. There is a story
they are weaving, across generations running
parallel to one another, they share a living dream,
in that building, on 12th and Polk Street,
behind the brick, yes, those words they etch
onto notebooks & the illuminated air
are incantations, summoning unthinkable
color from stone.

PLAINFIELD, NEW JERSEY

Spring Ploughing (43–70)

but if the earth has not been fertile it's enough to lift it
into song, I almost hear Virgil saying in the background
of my mind's moonlit vestibule, where the animals gather

to sift their dreams, weigh prophecy. There was more than one
messenger who said we must believe in spring: Bill Evans, Lucille
Clifton who chanted *the future is possible*, meant it, filled pages

with flowers to light our way home. In spring, we reap color, vibrance,
in every mode: lawns & leaves, the trunks of trees, our clothes,
birds racing forth out of winter's silver ambience into unabashed,

prismatic splendor. The greenness gathered over months
in the planet's subconscious, that gallant greenness
of newly discovered love, an imagination at work, like a tide

of green cascading up the cliffside, the green tendrils
& shoots & roots expanding their shadowed network, *rhizomatic*
schemata, they whisper in the graduate seminar, reading Deleuze,

and Guattari, that other philosopher of spring, who sang of three
ecologies: the land, the mind, and the people; the way the green
in me depends upon the green of the multitude for its strength

& proper form, consciousness an ever-expanding grove;
leaf, mud & stone; this slick, green infinity we hold, & keep,
if only we learn to adore the practice of its cultivation

the warmth of our sun overhead a kind of guiding ethos, the light
you give that annihilates or ushers into life. The way a curse is cast
by the same mechanism as a name, or a call to come back home,

where the trees of the field are an ensemble swaying, the melody
in the air ages older than any human sound, though you know it by heart.

EATONVILLE, FLORIDA

for Zora Neale Hurston

For our purposes, we begin with the eternal
feminine and its string of beads, end with you

as a girl in Eatonville, days before you board
a boat to cross the river, leapfrogging the invisible

partition that separates your hometown
from Jacksonville and its caverns full of cash;

the haywire soundscape you once adored,
and a private school scholarship to supercharge

your future. The tenor of the underlying metaphor
becomes clear only once I am older, preparing

to teach your essay to a classroom full of engineers,
their palms pressed directly to the pulse of whatever

our species is soon to become. Your journey was a map
of the modern mind's uncountable transformations:

traversing the water from home, a place named
for the man who helped your ancestors set its silver-gray

foundations, to the big city bearing a sigil of wholesale
slaughter, thousands destroyed in the name of a nation's

blood-drenched invention. Cosmic Zora, we call to you now
from across the flecked darkness, arms filled with pages

blank as bone, searching for the words we need
but cannot hold and remain as we are.

HAWTHORNE, CALIFORNIA

for the Beach Boys

What did I know of never-ending summer and surf
rock riffs to open the day? The sheer brightness
of Carl Wilson's falsetto running counter to the music's
melancholier revelations—*I may not always love you.*
The family band from Hawthorne, California, casting a line
from the mid-1960s into my living room, Tuesday afternoon
at the turn of the century via VH1, a rerun of *100 Best Albums*
of All Time showing in the three p.m. slot. And now *Pet Sounds*
is blaring through the corridors of our home somehow,
as my big sister recounts the school day's adventures
on the house phone upstairs, our mother already
on her way back from the city to check math homework
and ensure we are both still alive. But I am essentially
immovable at this point; newly initiated into a sound
I do not understand until I am old enough to be nostalgic
for windswept locales, and singular moments in time
I never lived through, though I know them, I can
assure you, in a place a thousand parsecs beyond
the limits of my present form.

ROLLING FORK, MISSISSIPPI

Irrigation (100–117)

and cover everything far and wide with a coat of mud,
that we might remember our source code & original
hymns: *humos*, humility, humor, human, humiliation.
All ways of getting back into the ground, reminders
of the dust we turn to once this step in our dance
is done. Muddy Waters wails: *well I wish I was a catfish*,
and the seed of that Ovidian lyric becomes the Rolling
Stones, Stevie Wonder hovering above a throne of luminous
computation, relaying the tale of father figures gathering
moss, long-departed, fugitive as the sounds of life our grand
-parents left in open fields, each colossal as autumn
skies appear to the intrepid eyes of children. We are
creatures of clay and air; breath & granular earth; iron,
carbon, rivers, dandelions in the DNA singing our bodies
photosynthetic, calling us toward the infinity we perceive,
if only in part, from this corner of the cosmic scatterplot:
all this obdurate loveliness we built down here in the muck.

HANOVER, NEW HAMPSHIRE

for Claude McKay

The wet mop glides like a dancer across the hardwood floor,
abolishing all traces of dirt, beer, blood, from last night's
battle royale. The man attached to it is a bard devoted
to lusher climates, vagabonds & folk songs, the foreseeable
aesthetic limits of a politics rooted in pain. He is here to write
and keep this house from falling asunder. To wash windows
downstairs, while chronicling the stretches of bright sempervirens
surrounding him now, in this clamorous corner of the New
Hampshire landscape. The Upper Valley in spring: graduation
only weeks away as he divides the days between this work
of cultivated spotlessness, and the lines which will usher him
into permanence, he imagines, if only he can capture the balance,
the swing, between leaping streams & the sound a zinc bucket
makes colliding against the ground. The dark waters waving
from side to side within its bounds, an ocean all his own.

CHAPEL HILL, NORTH CAROLINA

for George Moses Horton

What was held in the young man's thinking were concentric
worlds, angels' arrangements, relentless genius set loose
from the page's gray enclosure. Imagine the scene:
George's invisible compositions populate and then take hold
of the sunlit air, the college green in Chapel Hill his dedicated
stage, crowds gathering to hear the monumental bard hold court:
elegies and the outlines of birds, world-pictures of the landscape
that would outlive him. Not unlike the lines themselves, for years
etched only onto the space between passersby on the way to class,
an ancient art revived in the flesh of a prodigy in chains. Seventeen:
the same age as freshmen placing quarters at his feet as he sells the sounds
the engine in his head makes. And these in lieu of the produce he
is sent there to trade, which he wrestles from the earth with hands
and horse-drawn plough while sketching silently the image of the beloved
in his mind. One he has never met, but has been hired to celebrate
in song, which he will, once the colors and dimensions are perfected,
of the rooms he is building, in a place beyond matter no mortal can see.

SEATTLE, WASHINGTON

Star-Lore (204–258)

in memory of the 1995–1996 Seattle SuperSonics

and when the rising sun, with panting horses, first breathes on us,
our dreams fly off, alight on bedroom walls. There,
they await our return in grander forms, coordinated
during the day. Or so I speculate from adulthood's remove,
recalling summers I ran for hours along the street

with my neighborhood compatriots, who likewise
held in mind a superpowered self-portrait, unchained
by physical laws, lifting an arm or leg off the ground,
and ascension following as a logical next step.
The ancients had a name for these moments, where

such strange figurations entered language: *Adynaton*,
they called it, when hyperbole stretched toward the realm
of the impossible: animals tumbling from the sky, the Lake of Fire
draped in frost. How everyone I knew or read described Shawn
Kemp during the 1995–1996 NBA season, when the 6′10″ power

forward performed a range of miraculous feats in KeyArena,
"Reign Man," he was named, a play on the infamous
Seattle climate. His star point guard, Gary Payton,
was "the Glove"; chosen by a cousin, who once saw
him playing defense against the Phoenix Suns,

described the opposing guard as ensnared, captive
there, *a baseball in a glove*, and the moniker stuck,
just like "Reign Man," which resonates in seemingly

infinite directions once you hear it, then see it on paper:
King of Rain, King of Reins, riding cobalt stallions across

the horizon. In his prime, Kemp was limitless: baby hooks;
one-handed tomahawks with his left; a chest pass, heat
-guided, beams across half-court to the other big
man, Sam Perkins, who scored an easy two without
the ball touching the ground. So there was Kemp,

Payton, Perkins, and Detlef Schrempf, who averaged
a respectable 17 points, 5 assists, and 4 rebounds
that year before injuring his knee 63 games in, on 52 percent
shooting from the field, which still paled in comparison
to the clinic he would put on whenever I played *NBA Jam*

with my cousins and assorted strangers over the years, Shawn
& Detlef the game's chosen duo when you opted for the Sonics,
who also, you should know, have a compelling tale
as it pertains to names, theirs being chosen by a local boy
who wanted his selection to reflect the newest Boeing

airplane, the Supersonic Transport, or SST, which was planned
but never built, an abstraction that only ever found its place
in the world through the bodies and play of the team, which
existed for 41 years before becoming the Thunder of Oklahoma
City, where it also rains fairly often, 924 millimeters per year

to Seattle's 999, though the city is not as well known for this
atmospheric reality, and has never had a player called anything,
as far as I can tell, that has its roots in the local weather
report, or the sounds that zip through the sky from stone
-gray clouds, machines so swift they crack the invisible

blockades separating all we cannot perceive, except by its
shattering. Or the occasion of its repair, depending on how
you think about it, and if you're the kind of person who is inspired
by an early morning, where the first thing you hear is the storm.

ANCHORAGE, ALASKA

for Herbert Frisby

In dreams, I am the emperor of ice. A thousand white
wolves galloping through wave after wave of snowfall,
its shards like diamonds the size of dice. The dogs
are without names in this vision; almost imperceptible
against the silver landscape, but I call to them now, one
by one to fill the dark, my feet scaling mountains

without touching them. Ascending, I see Matthew Henson,
who once cut a figure in church calendars and hardback
children's books like no other, powder-flecked fur a halo
around his face. Unsmiling always, stalwart, an explorer
beyond the need for language or backstory, it seemed,
as if he had emerged in totality from some floe in the middle

of Antarctica, the first black man to hold the North Pole
in his glare, designed for the glory and dangers of life
below zero. The second was Herbert Frisby: biologist,
educator, Alaskan correspondent for the Baltimore
Afro-American, tracking meticulously all that called
to him from within the polar vastness.

It was Frisby who fought for years to see Henson credited
with discovering the North Pole in 1909, back when he
was still a college student at Howard, living in the lab, yet
to make his twenty-six trips to the Arctic, fly over the apex
of the known world, meet the president, chronicle atomic
testing on Amchitka Island, teach children for decades

to cast their looking toward the unseen, whether microscopic, or blanketed by winter, or obscured from the record until one dares to inscribe the names of our champions into the grand American Mythos with exactitude and grace, and thus catalog their footprints in the mud, and the grass, and the snow of History, refusing to relinquish what we are everywhere assailed for remembering.

WHITE SULPHUR SPRINGS, WEST VIRGINIA

for Katherine Johnson

The math in the girl's mind scales walls,
courses across the ceiling of her childhood home
in White Sulphur Springs, dances along the surfaces
as she walks from end from end, giving language
to the symbols. It was Lévi-Strauss who said
a certain genius for music & math lingers within
some of us from birth, that one hears the sounds
& sees the signs in ways defying description,
then elaborates that vision, or else allows it to lie
dormant: fading to background like a kind of fog or diegetic
instrumental, humming in the atmosphere of a single
life. But Katherine's parents saw the gift for what it was:
portal to another plane, a key to the invisible
architecture of oak trees & moonlight, goldfinches
hunting just beyond the window. Thus, they traveled
from town to town, in search of teachers for the child
visionary in their midst: college at fifteen, then NASA,
then ships soaring above our heads into endless ultraviolet before
returning to us, magnetized by the infinitude in her eyes.

DIAMOND, MISSOURI

Tools and Tasks (160–175)

I must tell of the sturdy countryman's weapons,
without which the crops could not be sown or grown:
by which of course I mean the voice of George
Washington Carver, communing with the God he loves
in the outer dark, by the big woods, where he whispered
psalms to the soil & experimental science echoed back.
New plans for cultivation, a strategy through which this
devastated earth might be restored, replenished, implored
to share its mineral wisdom. He once described the natural
world as an "unlimited broadcasting station," DJed by
divine consciousness; audible on this human plane if only
one lends their attention to the ordinary chatter of animals
& plants, the way the trees talk through their subterranean
circuits, but also right to us: in radiant shapes & forms, fruits & leaves,
those winged apostles who call in the sun from its blue room to sing.

BEAVER, UTAH

for Philo T. Farnsworth

Ark of starlight, polyphonic
talking book, boundless
choir floating past the grave.
Mama claims you emanate
unseen waves which vandalize
young minds, blur
inner eyes, chain
us to the whims
of advertisers
if we are not
vigilant, do not
balance the screen's
mesmeric cadence
and those better worlds
promised by books
in our bedrooms, middle
school science class, pews
where each hardcover
hymnal holds a history
of ascension. You harvest
attention: bestow language,
smooth regional accents
until we are untraceable,
indeterminate over
the phone, transformed by all
this unfiltered Americana
beamed into our homes,
our dreams, shaping
our opacity.

NEW HAVEN, CONNECTICUT

for Edward Bouchet

Your thesis becomes a kind of shadow
book, lost to us apart from barest details;
field, title, date of submission: experimental
physics, "On Measuring Refractive Indices,"
1876. The boy raised in antebellum
Connecticut grows up and goes to Yale,
where his father was once a janitor,
porter, enslaved, to study the way light
bends when it encounters a sycamore,
a riverbed, the outstretched fingertips
of a child in America living on a street
named for heroes she has never met, attempting
to enfold the sun in her fist, which is no larger
than the sparrow on the telephone wire bisecting
her sense of the heavens, carrying lamentations
of uncles and friends within its numberless
copper veins. Such wonderment was your object
of study and adoration. How, with a speed
and exactitude we cannot perceive as we
presently are, one thing transforms
into another.

BOSTON, BRAINTREE, CAMBRIDGE, MASSACHUSETTS

1.
Treatment of the Land (71–99)

who constantly works the ground, and orders the fields
should share in the black earth's blessed bounty,
the sprawling flora, of course, but the rhythm too,
the grasshopper's emerald soloing, wave after wave
of cicadas swaying in their timeless tempo, rabbits
thumping coded warnings, unseen scripts
intelligible only as improvised performance,
opaque as the ringed pathways of a redwood's interior
life. Who works the ground knows such things
in a place that is entirely armored; and much older
than our instruments for measuring time, place,
or sound: navigates the symbols the way one might
a beloved passage of text, inherited from elders
with hands the texture of reeds grown alongside
a river's rushing countenance. Who works the ground
inherits much the modern world cannot extract
with ease, sees order within the open, somehow,
tells of translucent nets, ever more intricate, holding
all we survey in place. Says accompaniment is the art
of everyday life. And I can no more separate myself
from the living corridors of these woods than you
can step outside your own electrified limits, the million
microscopic collisions keeping you here, with us,
those sparks sailing along each surface you glide across,
your body not entirely separable from the waxwings,
bumblebees, cypresses cycling into and out of our sight
-lines as we labor, and fail, to distance ourselves
from the source of the warmth that we seek.

2.

(style studies)

Is the sound storming forth from Joe Gordon's horn
his voice, or something more? Something more
or less immortal, permanent, transitive like
the shape of an eye, or the love of a neighbor
-hood baseball club? Is the arrangement of stars
above the hospital the night your son is born
the style of God? The arc of a blacksmith's hammer
swing, transmuting the liquid mass below
into blades for a collector, the cooled flat steel
not unlike the tracks underneath the Green
Line train downtown, burrowing through the tunnels
of Boston, whose subterranean web is the city's style,
in a way. The conglomerate style of architects
and politicians, whose style is manifest
in the way they speak to masses gathered
on blocks as clean, as filthy, as their style
of governance permits. Beauty or blight. Or both entwined
in a kind of high-stakes wrestling on the ground of Being,
is what some might call the style of a life. How
we manage the elegance we get, while held
in the vise grip of time. What we build
with our measure of sunlight.

3.

From this distance, the stretches of iron
scrap in the Monatiquot River resemble
the corrugated skeletons of giants. The books
in your washable paper bag were composed
by authors who could not imagine you as you
currently are, or were, or so you think, even

now, months away from the moment this image
first visited, if that is a fair way to describe
the electrical transfer, between the poet's mind
and the great waterways of this world, the volleying
back and forth between childhood and these
early stages of your everyday silvering. Your quiet
quests from the door, to the cleaners, to the ice
cream shop to write a syllabus on pretending.
Where much of what you mean to articulate
is that you lived, once, in a world so enchanted
that to explain its wonders to the uninitiated
would require new language, syntax, a system
of pictures, perhaps, and on the parchment
you inscribe a rough outline of the universe
as we know it: neutron stars, hills and rivers,
sprinters, sticky notes and ten-dollar rings, boxes
of chalk and shards of tourmaline, house keys,
business cards, books of architectural art where
half the cities come from dreams. Everything within
the boundaries of the paper exclaims, and is shimmering.

DETROIT, MICHIGAN

What filled our home was mountain ranges, ribbons
in the sky, both metaphors for adoration's incalculable
heights. The Temptations' philosophical musings
on the distance between our flesh and the transcendent
feeling a beloved incurs. The propellers in David
Ruffin's golden voice box whir: *Beauty's only skin-deep*.
At five years old I believe it, am transfixed, by the almost
mechanistic smoothness with which the band moves
on-screen, footage from the sixties, a color palette I cannot
recognize, as if the very fabrics of their garments have
been brightened by the passage of time, or holiness,
as we are barred from listening to anything that is not
gospel, my parents have already decreed, the only
exception, a rationale never explained, are these halcyon
voices engineered in small, carpeted rooms in midcentury
Detroit, with names that teach me the range of the noun form
& its superordinary treasures: the Supremes, Frankie Valli
and the Four Seasons, the Dynamic Superiors, the Chi-Lites,
and of course the Jackson 5, a family band, who my mother
saw in concert once, in Harlem, at the Apollo, in fact, which
was also the name of a Motown band, first called
Kryptonite, which I will learn years later, as I study
the traces of this historical accelerator of African American
erudition, where the songs of a people traveling epic distances
across the ash, in the wake of a great inferno following
their joy and everyday striving, were broadcast to the world
as witness: the sprawling, invisible record of resources we held
and honed in the midst of unthinkable constraint, a sound perfected
as we shaped a refuge just above the shadow of the Veil, where
we gather together, even still, in that soft and limitless blue.

NOGALES, ARIZONA

Storms (311–334)

for Charles Mingus

the vast earth trembles: the creatures run, and humbling terror
emanates from the drums and contrabass in tandem.
The titan from Nogales stands amidst the tumult draped

in sable, as tall as Dolphy is on the stool to his left. We're in
Belgium now, 1964, and the band is warming up the way
the sky sometimes swings to celadon, just before

a peal of thunder cracks the day. Then their roaring
elegance concretizes: the lines take on their shapes
in air, a variation on a theme they know and are building

in real time. Watch: how each man present offers a vision
then, visibly, ruminates, as they cycle into and out of this
labyrinth assembled with largely invisible materials, like pain.

William Matthews once said that Mingus was "big as a bus"
in 1960, at the Showplace downtown, when he was still just
a boy inscribing verses on yellow paper, in search of understanding,

and a place to sequester the dueling in his brain.
At fifteen, Gayl Jones wrote the words "my god is a black giant."
Just this morning, I thought, *Goliath was a hero to the ones who watched*

him grow, changed his clothes, sparred as cousins until
his strength grew unwieldy. 28 minutes in, there's a moment
where Dolphy is on the flute now, and Mingus's strumming

resembles, almost, an archer's release. Or the shaman's
gesture, before the world as we know it is transformed.

OKLAHOMA CITY, OKLAHOMA

for Ralph Ellison

The temptation is to begin with our man
in a hole in the ground, hoarding brightness.
Or the brother behind the stove at Chehaw
Station, who is as permanent as music.
But right now, at the front edge of autumn
just before dawn, I'm considering the freight
a name carries: the small brown boy in Oklahoma
named for our great philosopher of friendship,
fatherhood, America. My wife tells me that
back in Honduras, *Emerson* is a family name;
a quartet of cousins carrying the moniker across
centuries. The eldest of these would have been
your contemporary, Ralph. A world away, though
you were separated by only a road trip's distance,
both citizens of the black South, in a sense, once
you made your way to Tuskegee to study trumpet,
then traded in that dream for one of an integrated
literary tradition: a bigger room for our sacred bards
to wail in. And for you to listen in at the door,
attentive to where the lines of thought converge
and distance themselves. All that you might show
and prove, the luminous living sum of that congregated
genius, when the occasion arose to solo.

CORINTH, VERMONT

Ancient Maxims (176–203)

for Alexander Twilight

I can repeat many ancient maxims to you,
almost all of which would narrate the dance
between what we assemble with metal and stone

and the utterances that fill our hours like birds
let loose in a room. In ancient Rome, the term
for carpenter was *faber tignarius*: maker of beams.

In nominative determinism, you become what you are
named. A boy called Chip dreams of being a potato farmer,
or else, of reparative dentistry. Lily double-majors in botany

& creative writing, her dorm room filled with blossoms.
With a name like Twilight, what else were you to make
with your one precious life? The first of us to graduate

from college, or serve in a state legislature. School principal,
architect, minister. In stories I read from the time
I am small, God speaks the light first. The rivers

& rhododendrons, rose quartz & firefinches all
come later. His principal act is illumination.
In the first instance, He is a maker of beams.

Millennia pass, and God enters the Earth
as a carpenter, building chairs, tables, shelves
where you might place your favorite

glass. What manner of loveliness was imbued
into such ordinary objects? If a touch of the hem
of his garment could heal, what then of the structures

he worked on for hours, studying each angle and grain,
to actualize forms he saw in his mind, ages older
than the trees, and the metal, in the carving tools in his hands?

TALBOT COUNTY, MARYLAND

for Frederick Douglass

Our syllabus stages the course as a dynamic conversation
between the Western Canon & its discontents, conversants,
contributors & revisionists remixing core motifs, themes,
to sketch worlds the ones who love them made in the language
of a universal machine. Gwendolyn Brooks updates *The Iliad*
so it speaks to the everyday explosions held inside a Bronzeville
kitchenette; Homer's *Odyssey* finds new life in the bluish green
of Walcott's Caribbean, its tercets full of coral & lime, salt &
schooners weighted by the songs of ghosts. So of course we begin
with Douglass, his vexed love of animals, earth; the name
he chooses for himself, from a poem no less, Sir Walter Scott's
The Lady of the Lake, birthdate pulled from the void
as an act of kinship with Lincoln, his first autobiography
ending with a critique of Christianity & vaulting into verse,
a parody, he calls it, of the way *saints can sing, / Or praise the Lord*
upon the wing, / Who roar, and scold, and whip, and sting & conspire
to destroy. Who spoke of the bond between photography & oration,
how the truly gifted speaker could place an identical picture in the mind
of each audience member at once. Standing before the crowd, I think
of him, his studied metamorphoses. How he spoke the images
behind his eyes into colors we could carry & keep.

ST. PAUL'S PARISH, SOUTH CAROLINA

Before there is a country,
there are laws denying
the enslaved the right
to assemble, earn
money, grow food,
or write. The Negro
Act of 1740: ratified
a year after the Stono Rebellion—
led by an insurgent, Jemmy—
leaves twenty dead:
his collective of sixty either
killed by militia or sent
to the Caribbean
in chains. In reports
he is hailed by a different
name: *Cato.* And thus
the occasion is enshadowed
by other honorifics: Cato's *Revenge*
or *Conspiracy*, it is alternately
called, this violence
so disquieting it opens
a portal to another
plane. Another set
of questions now circling
this newest iteration of human
being forged in a land already
marked by conflagration and blood
and inexorable dignity
no earthly force yet imagined
can regulate, or quell.

GREAT FALLS, MONTANA

Weather Signs: After the Rain (393–423)

for Alma Smith Jacobs

wherever she flies, cutting the thin air with her wings,
we hear a call to study the Soul as illustrated
in print; literature as technology

of embodied memory; a black girl in Great Falls,
Montana, genius cultivated by the care of her parents:
Emma Riley, the gifted quilter, & Martin Luther

Smith, cook for the Great Northern Railway,
her inheritance both stillness & unrelenting
speed. A theme she carries into her career

at Talladega College, studying psychology
between shifts as a bookmobile librarian, traveling
the dirt roads of Alabama in what I imagine

as a small cobalt bus adorned with pages, our protagonist
riding solo to share the good news about the magnificence
a collection of poems holds within its brief scope,

the places a novella can take you in the quiet
moments just before equinox. Consider
the treasures she kept in tow: Melville,

Marlowe, Hurston, Dickinson, Whitman,
Fauset, Hughes & his blue sensibilities
whispering from the back of the vehicle,

leaping forth from the text as she rides,
mile after mile, to homes & parks & school
-grounds where children assemble

to hear the stories of continents they have never seen
echo forth from the stacks of ancient wisdom
she has preserved for them, & will for thousands

for decades to come, as she expands the breadth
of her journeying & her dream of the gift
of ascension for all.

CHICAGO, ILLINOIS

The Worship of Ceres (335–350)

for the Black Chicago Renaissance

while your whole choir of companions follow, rejoicing,
make the vision plain. Say the horizon holds
more than lack of room for dreams to stand on stilts
& dance or leap to ether. For dahlias & hollyhock
to bloom unchained, beautifying blocks wherein we lost
& lived outside the electrified gates of history. Or so we
were told, shown, in textbooks & two-dimensional images
running against the splendor in our grandmothers' memorized
fables, recited in holiday living rooms & vestibules of churches
they fashioned with brick & hymn & pitchers of punch
as red as sunflame glinting between skyscrapers, towering above
the streets our uncles cleaned & run & run toward each other on
into warmth or killing embrace. Thank you for lines of wonderment,
grace, pictures of our collective overcoming overwhelming the shadow of death
thank you Richard Gwendolyn Margaret for fortresses you built for us in the dark

PHILADELPHIA, PENNSYLVANIA

Weather Signs: Moon and Sun (424–460)

And it will do you more good still to remember, this,
bombs dropped onto city blocks
from helicopters, eleven killed, five children,
sixty-one homes collapsed to cinders, over
two hundred left homeless from the blaze
as Philadelphia police engaged their full-scale

offensive against the living dreams of MOVE,
which was not, it bears mentioning, an acronym,
but the announcement of an action plan held
in common by John Africa and his comrades,
who died that day or else survived ten thousand
rounds of ammunition emptied by the authorities

into 6221 Osage Avenue, where they lived four years before
inferno engulfed those rooms in which they slept, imagining
other ways of organizing human life, visions enshrined in song
and text by friends and strangers alike, including the wunderkind
Rhodes Scholar hoop star novelist who attended college ten minutes
away, and would chronicle their strife and striving five years later

in *Philadelphia Fire*, an effort to tell the story of what was lost
in that volcanic incursion of state repression into the everyday tempo
of a neighborhood on the cusp of a new century yet bound, in its
topography and tenor, to the chains of an antebellum understanding, color
as class as outcome cast in stone the moment you get here, your zip code
a predictive figure: the cell or the cubicle, the congressional seat, what

will it be, for the children born on the opposite
side of imperial largesse, technological advance moving
at a pace invisible, inscrutable, to all but a designated few
selected through tests and social programs to survive, perhaps,
the wave of what is coming. It is better we remember this
than forget: the bombs and the bullets and containers of gas

to make the air hazardous, in the shadow of Du Bois
and his dreams of the world on its way, students gathered
in his name a decade before, the voices crying out and silenced
by explosions which return, not as ghosts, but as flesh
and blood, and words in the mouths of the young
demanding the moon

ATLANTA, GEORGIA

A Prayer for Augustus's Success (498–514)

for Martin Luther King Jr.

neighbouring cities take up arms, breaking the laws
that bound them: impious Mars rages through the world:
as the boy reads Thoreau in a Morehouse classroom.
He's fifteen years old, skipped two grades, still
discerning the circuits that make up modern life.
In 1944, the sounds of warplanes punctuate
the air above London; Jim Crow is law in the city
where the boy is born & studies philosophy now,
sociology, religion, extending the reach of his mind's
aperture out beyond the persimmon trees & mountainous
distance. He listens. Not only for arguments, symbols,
but soundscapes beneath the signs, the way a single
phrase, the manner of its articulation, can shift
the polarity of a room, nation, world, universe
contracting like the breath of an orator, the material
of all we know & desire born from the Word ascending

KNOXVILLE, TENNESSEE

for Nikki Giovanni

The day Latoya's back from college, she carries a sign
-ed collection of poems in tow. A birthday gift: the poet
in the author photo bearing a forearm tattoo which reads,
plainly, *Thug Life*. Try to understand. We are products
of a home where Tupac & his colleagues were contraband,
the music entering our lives only through fugitive
maneuvers—mixtapes purchased on the underground
market & studied in the basement's navy murk,
house parties on Nepperhan where the speakers
are so loud it feels like you are floating. Which is all
a way of saying, there was a certain danger, and electricity,
to the exchange. You are forever her favorite. Even once
I become the family poet, and start to learn your lines
as a matter of course, on my way to a voice I can carry
onstage, adding my own quadrants of color to the quilt
you sewed with Sanchez, Killens, Pritchard, the New
York Community Choir, you know the crew, with whom
you recorded a spoken word gospel album for our grand
-parents, two of them, in fact, as reminders you remembered
those late November nights they kept the heat on.
The amethysts in their eyes. Near the end, your dreaming
turned toward Mars. Our bard of black love & revolutionary
violence now unrepentant in her concern for the dance
of the upper atmospheres, gas giants, asteroids, a sense
we must shift the scale of our attention, and in the process
live more joyously inside the truth that we are not only
enemy combatants, or lovers doomed by impermanence,
but something like choruses of starlight floating, one
toward another, giving form to the shadows

DANA, WYOMING

I am black because I come from the earth's inside.

—AUDRE LORDE, "COAL"

Underground the men war against air
and graphite dust to pull cash from black
earth for children they see once
the sky clicks to the same thick indigo they watch
for hours interred in the tunnels digging,
digging, deeper than the roots of tubers
and legumes they warm in iron
pots as black as ore or opera
notes echoing across a dark hall hundreds
of miles away from the men
of Dana, Wyoming
who appear in no photographs we
can access to honor even
in this moment their faces and names for
the record at least the black ink disintegrating
on yellowed parchment in a box in a room I imagine
somewhere we might discover out there
for ceremonial purposes at least to say
in death we give your names to sun & azure
surface of the morning today we lift a psalm
where you live in abundance

CINCINNATI, OHIO

Weather Signs: Terrestrial (351–392)

for Charles Henry Turner

And often the ant, beating out a narrow track,
brings eggs from an innermost nest, and a huge rainbow
drinks, and a great troop of rooks leaving the fields
beat their wings together densely, in ranks.
It was Charles who had a mind to study
these crowds of enigmatic laborers:
the unheralded strength and cognition
of bees, spiders, ants, how they pass
along critical information, pictures and pathways
of imminent peril, one to the other.
Stories too: lore of drones
and colonies past, the mythology
of ants knows no end, but continues
through the black conduit of their striving,
in spite of wintertime frost or the amusements
of giants, who mostly know little
of the ambitions of armies of planning
ants, the ant-world architects and civil
engineers, who first dream up those mammoth
structures some call mere obstruction.
Charles spent his pocket money
on experiments, the checks he earned
as a science teacher in Cincinnati,
to travel into this shrouded kingdom morning
after morning, eventually proving the bees
could see in color, that ants had a shared
store of recollection, maps of the world

exchanged over time, across
consciousness, no matter how
he reshaped the environment
around them. *Tournoiement de Turner*,
they called it, Turner's whirl, how
the ant-citizens would circle in elaborate
patterns once returned from foraging
for food, generation to generation,
updating relentlessly, discovering a way
to eradicate the barrier between a space
they knew primarily by its limits,
and the aspirations they were given
by those who had gone on before

HOT SPRINGS, SOUTH DAKOTA

Startup Raises $200 Million to Bring Back the Woolly Mammoth
reads the headline shining from the black glass surface
before I sleep. Colossal Biosciences, based in Texas,
is in the business of *de-extinction*, they say, recovering
the wilds of the past through modern methods. To conjure
the mammoth, they will extract its essential elements
from the DNA of Asian elephants, their closest living family.
The website offers a carousel of creatures who, likewise, are now
possible candidates for resurrection. Dodos, Tasmanian tigers,
species more recently vanished by the death-beam glare
of the dominant way: *More by any means.* Money as immortality's
other face. In Hot Springs, there is an archive of bones, a museum
devoted to Ice Age fossils, and the skeleton of the mammoth stands
above it all like a herald. In this moment, how can we say what is gone
and mourn it, or move on, learning from the wreckage left
in the wake of our avarice and envy? Who will stand at the gate
of our dreams and decide, if not us, who have grown quiet,
so distant we cannot hear each other over the sound
of the ground beneath us splintering

MINNEAPOLIS, MINNESOTA

for Prince

Arrangements of amethyst, clouds of lavender mist
emanate from the incandescent sage onstage as he narrates
the elsewhere he hails from at a pace best described
as *peripatetic*: kinesthetic genius unfolding behind
a white guitar, microphone stand, whatever metal medium
the bard selects to let this latest epic levitate through.
At Super Bowl XLI, he collaborates with the rainstorm.
Alongside MJ he shreds, goes shirtless, growls like a jaguar,
crashes a lamppost, yes, in blurred footage he is a violet silhouette,
violins pirouette in the background while the man paints
landscapes of fathomless desire. Though his art, in a way,
is the swing between release and restraint, that line in the air
where the human body breaks into orchard at the touch
of another. The thought of it, even: the sound that brings
the feeling home, to live with you, and transform what you once
held true into something more lovely, and strange.

LOUISVILLE, KENTUCKY

for Muhammad Ali

As emcee, initially: oratorical
colossus, speedster, dashing
across a room in the distance
between the snap of a light switch
& total blackness. Every backstep
jab is taut as harp-string. Roaming
specter, hover & sting. Then bastion
of peace. Our shining dignity. Royalty,
still, despite the gold they stole. Then
solid granite, immovable, like striking
the hillside with open hands,
expecting movement. As statesman,
Prometheus. As poet, immortal, though
quieter now: as snowfall, or blade, or
birdsong in the mind of the flock as it flies.

AUDACIOUS, NEBRASKA

I'm trying to build a black utopia from scratch,
and thus find myself studying bygone attempts:
towns with names like Promised Land;
Africatown; Audacious, Nebraska, originally
known as DeWitty, as in Miles DeWitty, who
founded the post office there, alongside which
stood a church, three schools, a baseball team
called the North Loup Sluggers, after the river
which covers one-fifth of the state. The picture
on my desk is the color of fire. In it, a man named
George Riley stands with his team uniform on,
the shadow of the ball cap brim over his eyes
insufficient to protect us from the deliberate
strength, or else indifference, of his glare.
In another image, a hundred-plus gather
to watch that afternoon's game, backs turned,
while strangers on the Internet argue over who
they might have been based on various clues:
whose grandfather liked to smoke a pipe, the shape
of an overcoat, the way a human body holds itself
in space, and how such quiet choreographies
are transmitted in the blood.

GARY, INDIANA

for the Jackson 5

Before the boys unlock a pocket dimension to pop
stardom once unimagined, even by the standards
of post-Cold War American entertainment—its
excesses and unchecked exorbitance—they are brothers
in a studio in steel town Indiana, working on steps
for the twentieth time. Before MJ's robot remaps the range
of human movement, there is daylong practice, local talent
shows, each newly arrived sibling finding their place
in the ensemble, like an enjambed phrase in a poem
keeping the idea alive. Such was the electricity
of those early rehearsals in Gary, which I have seen
in the theatre of my imagination over the course of three
decades: first, in the late '90s with my parents and sister,
watching a made-for-TV film about the Jacksons
as a kind of collective cultural ritual, then as witness
to the destruction and rewards of a life devoted
to a single pursuit, where flawlessness is not so much
a useful abstraction, or motivating principle floating
at the horizon's edge, but the lone true baseline,
what we are here to accomplish, or else be destroyed
in the process of its glorious possession.

BOULDER, COLORADO

for Alonzo Clemons

Adamic impulse electrified,
propelled to the edges
of mortal speed. In clay
and bronze the quiet maker
conjures what he sees:
oxen, elephants, the unicorn's
horn a dagger pointing
at the margins of a blue
and white photograph.
Alonzo calls the one of dolphins
leaping, miniature stretch of cerulean
sea surrounding them, "Family Gathering."
Hippo Momma stands with her young.
Sledgehammer the Moose overlooks
his pedestal with invincible pride.
Is it pure replication he offers us,
or yet untold machinations of the mind?
In his eyes, the world is still
salvageable, can be remade
in an instant, alive
again, permanent.

HAILEY, IDAHO

for Ezra Pound

1.

The gentle art of making enemies

is what Frost once called

your expertise, this life

-long habit of doubling

the distance between yourself

and another with a word. You return

to me now, Ezra, split across

images: on the green of an asylum yard with Elizabeth Bishop;

letters with Langston Hughes where you say black voice

is the best thing black people have, so you hate

when you hear one talk

like a Harvard sophomore;

penning cantos in a silver cage.

2.

In deepest grief,

one of your lines comes to me: *what thy lovest well*

is thy true heritage. Is it true, old man? Madman,

fascist, chimera. Loved enough to be rescued

from your own mind. Your lawyer says

the poems are proof you walk between

worlds. You are nowhere

& everywhere now. An impulse dispersed

throughout the age, with no music

to contour its force.

3.

Timeworn destroyer, what of yours can we keep?

What gift survives

the man? To make you an exception

is to deny your children, who blanket the earth

in ashes.

MILWAUKEE, WISCONSIN

for Christopher Latham Sholes

An error carries its pinch of pain,
but is not permanent,
with a typewriter. It gestures toward

a way of life. Consider that classic
opening of those interviews with poets
you love: *what do you write with or on,*

and the history of typewriters
embedded in it.
Ashbery's typewriter came to him

as a kind of fix, while writing a poem with lines so long he finds himself
forgetting the ends of them, just before landing.
He compared the machine's speed

to his pace with a pen, the long dance of mind and hand,
made the switch for life. A. R. Ammons's
was an Underwood, manual, that he bought in Berkeley

in the 1950s, kept for the control it allowed
him over the spaces and shapes he called
to the page like an ellipsis of birds

in earshot. Praise the instrument, extension, apprentice,
vessel through which the ink and music roil
to make this new third thing that enchants

us, holds the law within its dimensions, moves soldiers
over continents, houses vows which lived once
only in the heart and air. Is cognition

made real. To be torn, kept, cherished as it moves
from paper to tesselations of dust, back to the green
and black earth which is the body of the Lord.

CEDAR RAPIDS, IOWA

for George Nissen

We all dreamed of trampolines, or else
their second-order effects. Engineered them

wherever core elements could be found: an old mattress
at the back of our building; solid ground; that soft

bright surface in a McDonald's PlayPlace
from which you could float for the breadth

of the beat between the scene in your mind of the leap
and the leap itself, where you are airborne, illuminated,

quickly immortal. In Cedar Rapids, George crafts a prototype
in Mom and Dad's garage, inspired by circus performers,

set on the dream of general levitation. Soon, he will
found his own tumbling and trampoline company

with an old coach, aiming to mass-produce
his magical device, this window into the world

of hummingbirds, daydreams, and other hovering
things. *Trampolín*: Spanish for diving board, blur

bridging the blue of sky and pool, spring
and spin, step and float, fall, fly.

PORTLAND, MAINE

for Macon B. Allen, the first black man to practice law in America, and countless others

To celebrate the first is also, always, to honor absence. Depth and breadth of the void before: all those who might have been what, where, you are now, if not for the fences, fictions, invisible traps set between our beloved and the future. So we suit up to dive. Scale the sky. Bridge the distance between the soil and stars, Stars and Stripes, suns and moons, sons and daughters who fall too soon from flights our elders could not fathom. Airless heights beyond the blue. We dart through perfect darkness. In search of you.

ALBUQUERQUE, NEW MEXICO

for Jay Wright

The literal has its place

& patrons. But I most admire

those who say

it's symbols the whole way

down. There was a bond,

I am told, of Bronze Age believers

who claimed to hold the resurrection

within themselves: Their slain

teacher & friend returned to them

only through recitation, in word

and act, of his magnetic example.

In poems, you grant us

a grammar for the universal, guide

us to that far point in the desert

where maker and made converge, blur,

their unchecked splendor

electrifying the expanse.

PORTLAND, OREGON

(owed to the Phillips-head screwdriver)

You return him to me as he was,
asking for you from the half-shadow
of the kitchen cabinet. Or stooped,
slightly, over a piece of particle board
furniture upstairs, broken through playtime
collision between it & one of his children,
the force of sheer duration. I'm trying
to remember if he ever actually said the word
screwdriver, but I don't think so. No, usually
it was some version of *Pass me the Phillips-head*,
and the man was off to work: tinkering with the boiler,
my toy robot, our carousel of disrepair never slowed.
But he remained there, always, you too, opening the door
for the involvement of another, this small boy
to have a place in the design, working diligently
to fix what he could neither reach nor see.

GALVESTON, TEXAS

(Juneteenth sonnet)

Is not this delayed news of freedom's arrival, in itself,
a description of the deliverance on offer?
One that bends, shape-shifts to meet the needs of its fashioner.
Saidiya Hartman once described emancipation
as a *nonevent*: a sense she shares with George Jackson,
who likewise renders the cage on paper. I've been
attempting to wrestle it into prose, this pursuit
of a liberation exceeding the material, its jagged
constraints, an account of how it feels to be here, in this
body, tripled. The interval between ancestral past and present
animated by anguish, knowing you are never only
yourself, but a fantasy walking, invisible the way
Ellison meant it: not to say no one sees you standing
there, but rather, that what they see is entirely invented.

HUNTER, NORTH DAKOTA

(in praise of the Kodak camera)

Album after album, she stacks the images
on both wooden end tables, which we polish
with Pledge until they shine like shields.
Which they are, after all, in a sense: our defense
against forgetting, and decay. Her fleet of red
and yellow Kodak cameras could fill a small silo,
so adept was my mother at gathering transience
with the flash emitting from her right eye.
That portion of time now held in her pocket
until our trip to CVS, where a crew of alchemists
no older than my sisters would summon
pictures from the dark of us, making the past
more textured, beautifully unfamiliar.
It was never magic to me. Only ordinary, artful
science, though I still recall a single snapshot,
with our crème and turquoise couch
all covered with birds, where it's my mother
and father and me, and I'm there at the midpoint
of their glancing into the lens,
a living collision of them: her eyes and smile,
his posture as I stood, looking off just beyond
the photographer's shoulder, the machine
in her hands building monuments from paper and light.

NEW ORLEANS, LOUISIANA

with a line from Sunni Patterson

We know this place: this power, this pain.
This art, this armor, this ardor, each other.
Both the premise and promise of the music is this:
that the human voice is home
to untold treasures; can be dispersed
and split, knit to drum kits,
sped up to splintering, and yet preserve
a portion of its warmth. The Soul persists.
We bounce like light to lift the world.

WADSWORTH, NEVADA

for Gwendolyn Bennett

Before it breaks: Before Joshua Bennett flees
across the country with his baby girl in the back seat,
before Harlem or D.C., before "The Song
of Hiawatha" sung in an atrium full of artwork,
before Paris with Stein, before Hemingway,
before Wright and Hughes knew her,
before first marriage in Florida, or tragedy,
or triumphant debut; before claret flames
embossed in ink, lunar odes in stanzas dancing clean
across the zeitgeist, before spies, or separation, or white
-collar lies that divide a family three and four times over,
there is a father. And a mother. And a girl in Nevada
who live together, fresh from Giddings, Texas. Parents
hired by the Bureau of Indian Affairs to teach,
daughter already showing signs of the genius
that would illuminate a century. Though her name
would soon be obscured, we sing it now, and not
for the first time: *Gwendolyn*, who shines
like the notes of a vibraphone, each swing
of the player's mallet shifting twilight's shade.

EVERYWHERE, DELAWARE

There are more chickens than people
in the state of Delaware. Here too.
Out by the blue shed, they sing &
run & strut in sunlight,
our chestnut-carmine quintet:
Big Tony, Tessa, Lillibet,
Pynchon, & Marigold, who glows
just like one. At dawn, the chicken wire
is the same silver as the hounds
with whom they share this green
territory. The province of robins,
rabbits bounding across the summer
sidewalks, much faster than those princely
turkeys, who are guarded by law.
What a world. Revenge & ritual, tooth & claw,
wing, maw, eyes that expose the bribe
& lie of our separateness, the hollow
dominion we are taught to worship.
Blessed be the fleet & angular
beasts whose whoop & howl
& hoot & caw infuse
the day with harmony.
They are what metaphor
aspires toward & does
not reach. Each reminding
us: the beauty of strength
is mercy.

LITTLE ROCK, ARKANSAS

for the Little Rock Nine

June Jordan says children
are the way the world begins
again and again. In decades
-old images I see an endless assembly
of them, choreographing what lies ahead.
Is it will, or attunement to the Geist,
prophetic sight to pursue this pathway
through Jim Crow's caging of matter
and mind? My father says they decide
over dinner: he will be the one to go
to school across town, cut the color line
in two. How often it is the young and unheralded
who form this history, make it more than a litany
of wars. The chorus calls to us through an expanse
of gray, marching, marching, their clarion witness
turning the earth.

PROVIDENCE, RHODE ISLAND

(self-portrait in the future, where at least two dreams come true)

The kids are as tall as the heads of hills. They reach upward
with their cinnamon arms to pull classics from the shelves,
one title at a time, for their father, who is so old now there is platinum
running through his beard, like Walt Whitman in the moonlight.
Can you hear the dogs? Apollo 6, Atlas, Artemis, galloping across
the illuminated grass, a story in three parts. Vinyl remains in vogue.
The black record spins, and Sarah Vaughan fills the living room
as we float from corner to corner, our souls glistening through
our shirts. The azaleas out front so bright, from afar you might
mistake them for a cut of dusk, stolen by mercenary men with eyes
for such rare memorabilia. But they are only flowers. My most recently
discovered superpower is an inordinate leaping ability, which allows
me to bound to afternoon activities along the roofs of neighbors; the dust
from their chimneys darkening my New Balances to gray. Linger with me,
here, on this day. My pockets replete with astonishments. The sky
as smooth as that skipping stone in your palm the second before it flies.

KAHALU'U BAY, HAWAII

(a companion history of surfing)

1.

The first known account of surfing was written during the 1640s in what is now Ghana. Surfing was independently developed from Senegal to Angola. Africa possesses thousands of miles of warm, surf-filled waters and populations of strong swimmers and sea-going fishermen and merchants who knew surf patterns and crewed surf-canoes capable of catching and riding waves upwards of 10 feet high.

—KEVIN DAWSON

Our ways with water are ancient & invincible:
In the 17th century, kids on the Gold Coast
ride longboards that are twelve feet long, scaling the crests
of waves, aimed at oceanic zones unreachable
otherwise, outside such strange & elegant mastery,
this lilt & lean & lightest touch. "Counting the seas,"
they would call it, this blue vision, this sense of when to
paddle in, forge ahead or exit, to commune with gods
who cultivated kingdoms there, in the dark frenzied motion
just offshore, where our eyes meet the edge of the eternal.

2.

The perpetual fear is contamination: swimming pools, drinking
fountains, the touch of a hand that is mostly water. The brain too:
Lightning and rain. Surf-canoes were made from cottonwood trees

said to be sacred, to hold the souls of children who had not yet arrived. Ancestors walked through the world below. The board was a bridge. Language is only one way we walk across.

3.

The city in the sky Daniella paints
has a dance studio, plant nursery, bodega,
used bookseller, two children floating
as they play Go Fish, a mom-and-pop outfit
called Surf Shack, where you buy boards
that sail through the air like seraphim.
The streets are named for birds
of prey. The water levitates like everything
else, and there is no word in the common
tongue for falling.

TOPEKA, KANSAS

Appropriate Times for Tasks (259–310)

for Gwendolyn Brooks

The Moon herself has set certain days as auspicious
such as the ones where Gwendolyn's father,
David, builds a mahogany bookshelf
for his beloved. The day he brings it to her
as a wedding present. And the dark mornings
he pores over tomes his daughter would place in that sacred
frame: Harvard Classics, mostly, Homer & Aeschylus,
Plato, Seneca. Ancient names embossed in gold,
shimmering against worn hardback covers,
each as green as the grass on a grave.

The groves in her eyes, they are growing
now, beyond the bounds of the apartment,
outward and up into space. *Out of the bloom*,
a friend of a friend, Chrysanthemum, says,
omitting blueness, altering the phrase's circuitry,
for reasons I can understand even at a distance.
As a teenager, Brooks translates the *Aeneid*,
whole passages from the original Latin,
eventually crafting her own parodic verse,
timeless in its effervescent rage:

Forgive me this small speech, wherein I rave
That thou didst ever live to harass me.
Oh, not that I do not appreciate
The mild, concordant beauty of your lines—
But I am puzzled by them; I translate,
And every word seems but a set of signs.

Out of the blue, we say sometimes
because we imagine the truth
careening through the atmosphere
like a winged beast, to interrupt

our boredom, or our fear. Or is it
because we were borne from the sea,
and call back to that origin even
still, the Unconscious orchestrating
our idioms as we sleep, pointing home.
She titles the poem
"To Publius Vergilius Maro,"
direct as the arrow
in an assassin's dream: a missive
to the long-buried bard
who speaks with her now, only

through language we call dead as a matter
of specificity, though she summons
his audible sense of things in the act
of composition. Unearthing a voice that is both
hers & altogether new, fugitive,
like the name of the Almighty.
In those days, Gwendolyn turns toward endlessness
to call in a manner not of speaking
per se, but of perceiving the distance
between the words one etches onto the air

& the whirlwind, compelling that stillness within us to move.

AUTHOR PHOTO BY JOSHUA TAYLOR

Joshua Bennett is the author of eight books of poetry, criticism, creative nonfiction, and children's literature, including *The Sobbing School* (Penguin, 2016), winner of the National Poetry series and a finalist for the NAACP Image Award; *Being Property Once Myself* (Harvard University Press, 2020), winner of the MLA's William Sanders Scarborough Prize; and *Spoken Word: A Cultural History* (Knopf, 2023), which was named a *New York Times* Notable Book of 2023 and a Best Book of the Year by *The New Yorker*.

Dr. Bennett earned his PhD in English from Princeton University and an MA in Theatre and Performance Studies from the University of Warwick, where he was a Marshall Scholar. He has recited his original works at the Sundance Film Festival, the NAACP Image Awards, and President Obama's Evening of Poetry and Music at the White House. For his creative writing and scholarship, he has received fellowships and awards from the Guggenheim Foundation, the Whiting Foundation, the Institute for Advanced Study, the National Endowment for the Arts, and the Society of Fellows at Harvard University.

Alongside his work as an academic and author, Bennett is the founder and principal of Solon, a design practice specializing in the art of adaptation. He is also the founding editor of The Duke Poetry Series: A Duke University Press imprint devoted to the conversation between poetry and literary criticism. He lives in Massachusetts with his family.

PENGUIN POETS

GAROUS ABDOLMALEKIAN
Lean Against This Late Hour

PAIGE ACKERSON-KIELY
Dolefully, A Rampart Stands

JOHN ASHBERY
Selected Poems
Self-Portrait in a Convex Mirror

PAUL BEATTY
Joker, Joker, Deuce

JOSHUA BENNETT
Owed
The Sobbing School
The Study of Human Life
We (the People of the United States)

TED BERRIGAN
The Sonnets

LAUREN BERRY
The Lifting Dress

JOE BONOMO
Installations

PHILIP BOOTH
Lifelines: Selected Poems 1950–1999
Selves

JIM CARROLL
Fear of Dreaming: The Selected Poems
Living at the Movies
Void of Course

SU CHO
The Symmetry of Fish

ADRIENNE CHUNG
Organs of Little Importance

RIO CORTEZ
Golden Ax

MARISSA DAVIS
End of Empire

ALISON HAWTHORNE DEMING
Genius Loci
Rope
Stairway to Heaven

CARL DENNIS
Another Reason
Callings
Earthborn
New and Selected Poems 1974–2004
Night School
Practical Gods
Ranking the Wishes
Unknown Friends

DIANE DI PRIMA
Loba

STUART DISCHELL
Backwards Days
Dig Safe

STEPHEN DOBYNS
Velocities: New and Selected Poems 1966–1992

EDWARD DORN
Way More West

HEID E. ERDRICH
Little Big Bully

ROGER FANNING
The Middle Ages

ADAM FOULDS
The Broken Word: An Epic Poem of the British Empire in Kenya, and the Mau Mau Uprising Against It

CARRIE FOUNTAIN
Burn Lake
Instant Winner
The Life

AMY GERSTLER
Dearest Creature
Ghost Girl
Index of Women
Is This My Final Form?
Medicine
Nerve Storm
Scattered at Sea

EUGENE GLORIA
Drivers at the Short-Time Motel
Hoodlum Birds
My Favorite Warlord
Sightseer in This Killing City

DEBORA GREGER
In Darwin's Room

ZEINA HASHEM BECK
O

TERRANCE HAYES
American Sonnets for My Past and Future Assassin
Hip Logic
How to Be Drawn
Lighthead
So to Speak
Wind in a Box

NATHAN HOKS
The Narrow Circle

ROBERT HUNTER
Sentinel and Other Poems

MARY KARR
Viper Rum

W. B. KECKLER
Sanskrit of the Body

JACK KEROUAC
Book of Blues
Book of Haikus
Book of Sketches

JOANNA KLINK
Circadian
Excerpts from a Secret Prophecy
The Nightfields
Raptus

JOANNE KYGER
As Ever: Selected Poems

ANN LAUTERBACH
Door
Hum
If in Time: Selected Poems 1975–2000
On a Stair
Or to Begin Again
Spell
Under the Sign

PENGUIN POETS

CORINNE LEE
Plenty
Pyx

PHILLIS LEVIN
May Day
Mr. Memory & Other Poems

PATRICIA LOCKWOOD
Motherland Fatherland Homelandsexuals

WILLIAM LOGAN
Rift of Light

J. MICHAEL MARTINEZ
Museum of the Americas
Tarta Americana

ADRIAN MATEJKA
The Big Smoke
Map to the Stars
Mixology
Somebody Else Sold the World

AMBER McBRIDE
Thick with Trouble

MICHAEL McCLURE
Huge Dreams: San Francisco and Beat Poems

ROSE McLARNEY
Colorfast
Forage
Its Day Being Gone

DAVID MELTZER
David's Copy: The Selected Poems of David Meltzer

TERESA K. MILLER
Borderline Fortune

ROBERT MORGAN
Dark Energy
Terroir

CAROL MUSKE-DUKES
Blue Rose
An Octave Above Thunder: New and Selected Poems
Red Trousseau
Twin Cities

ALICE NOTLEY
Being Reflected Upon
Certain Magical Acts
Culture of One
The Descent of Alette
Disobedience
For the Ride
In the Pines
Mysteries of Small Houses

WILLIE PERDOMO
The Crazy Bunch
The Essential Hits of Shorty Bon Bon

DANIEL POPPICK
Fear of Description

LIA PURPURA
It Shouldn't Have Been Beautiful

LAWRENCE RAAB
The History of Forgetting
Visible Signs: New and Selected Poems

BARBARA RAS
The Last Skin
One Hidden Stuff

M.S. REDCHERRIES
mother

MICHAEL ROBBINS
Alien vs. Predator
The Second Sex
Walkman

PATTIANN ROGERS
Flickering
Generations
Holy Heathen Rhapsody
Quickening Fields
Wayfare

SAM SAX
Madness

ROBYN SCHIFF
Information Desk: An Epic
A Woman of Property

WILLIAM STOBB
Absentia
Nervous Systems

MAKSHYA TOLBERT
Shade is a place

TRYFON TOLIDES
An Almost Pure Empty Walking

VINCENT TORO
Hivestruck
Tertulia

PAUL TRAN
All the Flowers Kneeling

SARAH VAP
Viability

ANNE WALDMAN
Gossamurmur
Kill or Cure
Manatee/Humanity
Mesopotopia
Trickster Feminism

JAMES WELCH
Riding the Earthboy 40

PHILIP WHALEN
Overtime: Selected Poems

PHILLIP B. WILLIAMS
Mutiny

MIA S. WILLIS
the space between men

ROBERT WRIGLEY
Anatomy of Melancholy and Other Poems
Beautiful Country
Box
Earthly Meditations: New and Selected Poems
Lives of the Animals
Reign of Snakes
The True Account of Myself as a Bird

MARK YAKICH
The Importance of Peeling Potatoes in Ukraine
Spiritual Exercises
Unrelated Individuals Forming a Group Waiting to Cros